Christmas Cat Knitting Projects

Knitting Ideas for Cat at Christmas

Copyright © 2021

All rights reserved.

DEDICATION

The author and publisher have provided this e-book to you for your personal use only. You may not make this e-book publicly available in any way. Copyright infringement is against the law. If you believe the copy of this e-book you are reading infringes on the author's copyright, please notify the publisher at: https://us.macmillan.com/piracy

Christmas Cat Knitting Projects

Contents

Cats Love Sweaters 1
Christmas Bear & Cat Baubles 9
Santa Cat Hat 17
Santa Claws Cat 23
Cat Scarf Knitting Pattern 28
Easy Cat Toy Knitting Pattern 31
Knit Cat Mini Christmas Sleep Stockings 35
Make Your Own Knit Cat Bed 38
Fair Isle Mice – Pattern For Cat 50

Christmas Cat Knitting Projects

Cats Love Sweaters

Pattern for a custom fitted long sleeve turtleneck cat sweater. Since this pattern is meant to be custom fitted to your cat using the yarn and gauge of your choice, there is a little bit of math involved. If you find that your numbers don't work out perfectly, don't sweat it! Just fudge them a little, don't let math get in the way of the funny. Also, cats are bendy, squishy and generally confused by being measured, do the best you can. Close enough is close enough, the ribbing is pretty forgiving.

MATERIALS

– Any type of yarn will do, just choose your needle size as appropriate to the yarn weight.

– Set of double pointed needles or circulars

– Tapestry needle for weaving in ends

ABBREVIATIONS

CO = Cast on

BO = Bind off

Christmas Cat Knitting Projects

K = knit

K2T = knit two together

SSK = slip 2 stitches individually as if to knit, then knit those 2 stitches together

sts = stitches

2×2 rib = all ribbing in this pattern is *K2, P2* repeat to end of round.

DIRECTIONS

Knit a gauge swatch

CO 20 or so stitches and knit a few rows in stocking stitch then measure the gauge and jot it down.

___ Stitches per inch

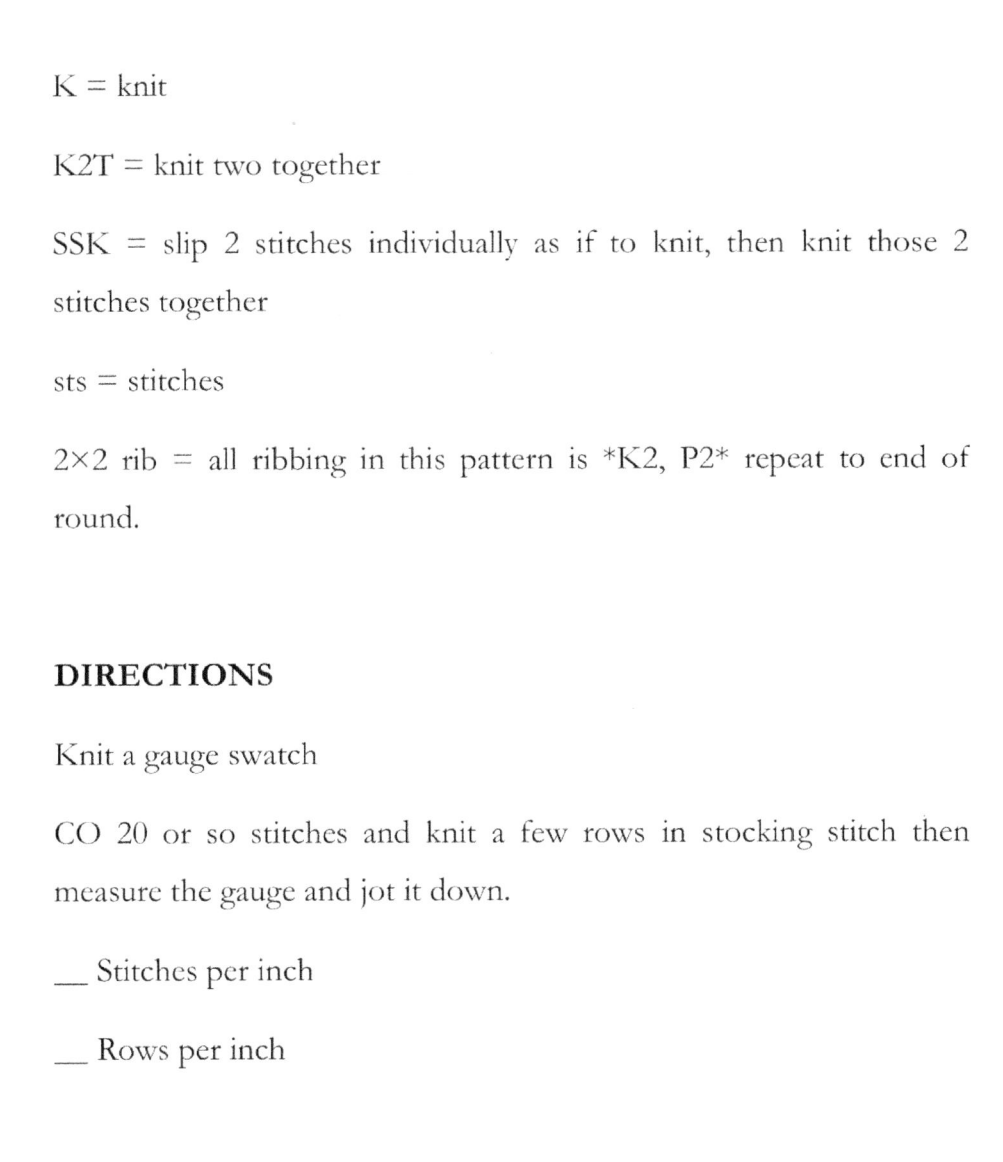

___ Rows per inch

Measure the cat

Christmas Cat Knitting Projects

__ Length from collar to start of back legs

__ Length between back and front legs

__ Distance between front legs

__ Width of front legs when looking at the cat in profile

__ Circumference of belly

__ Circumference of collar

__ Height of front legs

A little math

__ A = Circumference of belly x Stitches per inch, rounded to nearest number divisible by 4

__ B = Length between back and front legs x Rows per inch

__ C = Distance between front legs x Stitches per inch, rounded to nearest number divisible by 2

__ D = Width of front legs x Rows per inch

Christmas Cat Knitting Projects

__ E = (Length from collar to start of back legs − Length between back and front legs − Width of front legs) x Rows per inch

__ F = Circumference of collar x Stitches per inch

__ G = A−F

__ H = If G/2 is greater than or equal to E, H=1. Else H=E/(G/2), rounded to the nearest whole number

__ I = (Height of front legs − 1 inch) x Rows per inch

Belly

CO A and join for working in the round. Knit in 2×2 rib for B rounds.

Divide for arms

Continuing in 2×2 rib, work back and forth on C stitches for D rows, this will be the material that runs between the cats front legs. It will be referred to as the chest piece. Cut yarn leaving a tail to weave in later.

Join yarn and work the rest of the stitches in 2×2 rib for D rows, this will be the material that goes over the cats back.

You should now have a tube that splits for the arms and is of equal length chest and back.

Join for neck

Resume knitting in the round in 2×2 rib, complete 1 round.

Continue knitting in rib while decreasing for neck. To decrease: K2tog right after chest piece and SSK right before chest piece every H rounds until F stitches remain.

Knit ribbing for 1 more inch, BO loosely.

You can stop here and weave in ends for a nice fitted cat vest, or continue on to the sleeves…

Sleeves

Pick up and knit D stitches along each side of an arm slit starting at the point closest to the cats bum (total stitches = D x 2). Knit 1 round in 2×2 rib. Continue knitting in rib while decreasing every other round by K2tog at beginning of round and SSK at end of round until (2 x stitches per inch) remain, then continue knitting in rib until I rows total for sleeve have been completed. BO loosely.

Repeat for second arm.

Finishing

Weave in ends. Wrestle the sweater onto the cat. Laugh and laugh at the ridiculousness of it all.

Christmas Cat Knitting Projects

Christmas Bear & Cat Baubles

Materials :

50gm 8ply / DK for the body.

Small amount 8ply / DK in 2 colours for hat.

3.25mm knitting needles for body

4.00mm knitting needles for hat.

Christmas Cat Knitting Projects

Fibre filling

Black embroidery cotton & black, pink yarn for features.

2 beads for bear eyes

Christmas Bauble - the ones I used were aprox 19cm circumference.

Hot Glue gun.

Instructions.

For Bear Body

Make a front & back.

Using 3.25mm needles & bear colour cast on 38sts.

Christmas Cat Knitting Projects

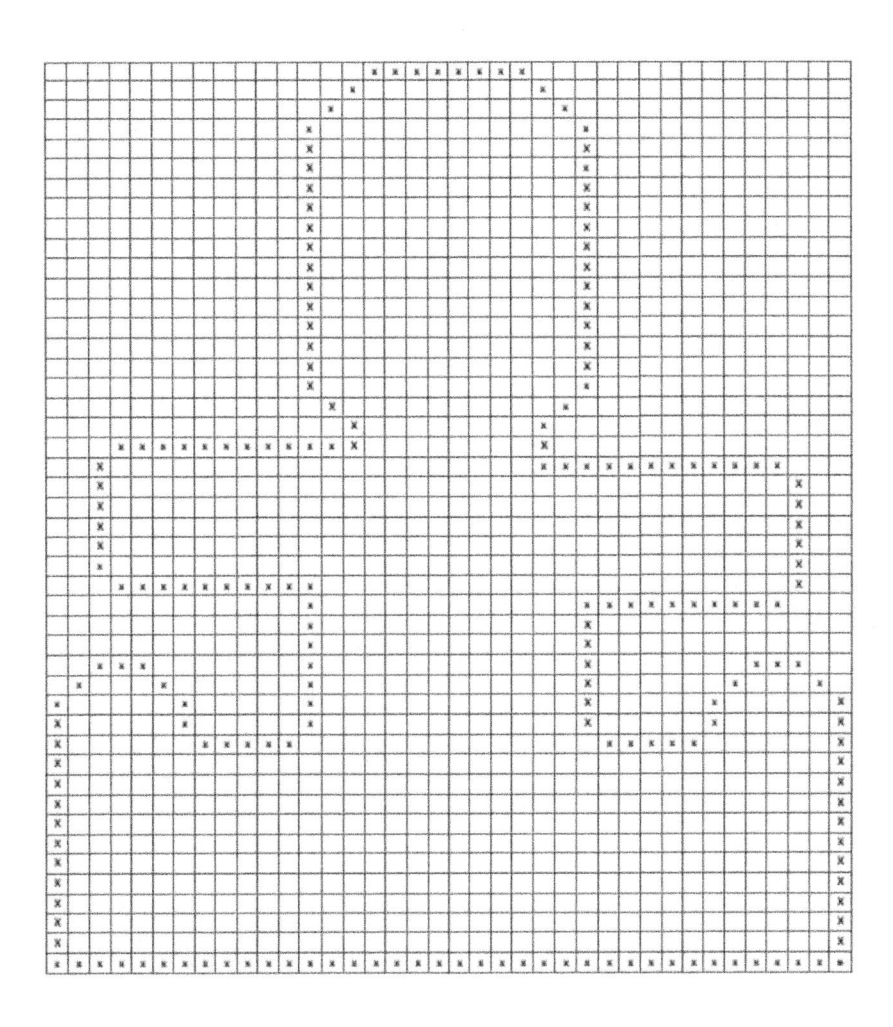

Starting at the bottom right hand corner, read from right to left, first row, then back left to right for second row etc.

Stitch the bear pieces together on the outside (don't do a seam then

Christmas Cat Knitting Projects

turn right side out) leaving a gap at the bottom for stuffing.

Stuff the head fairly firmly, but only stuff the body, arms & legs very very lightly & sew up open seam. Because the bear wraps around the bauble & is hot glued, you only need a small amount of stuffing.

Even here in this photo, I've stuffed the body too much & had to squish it flat a bit, so stuff less.

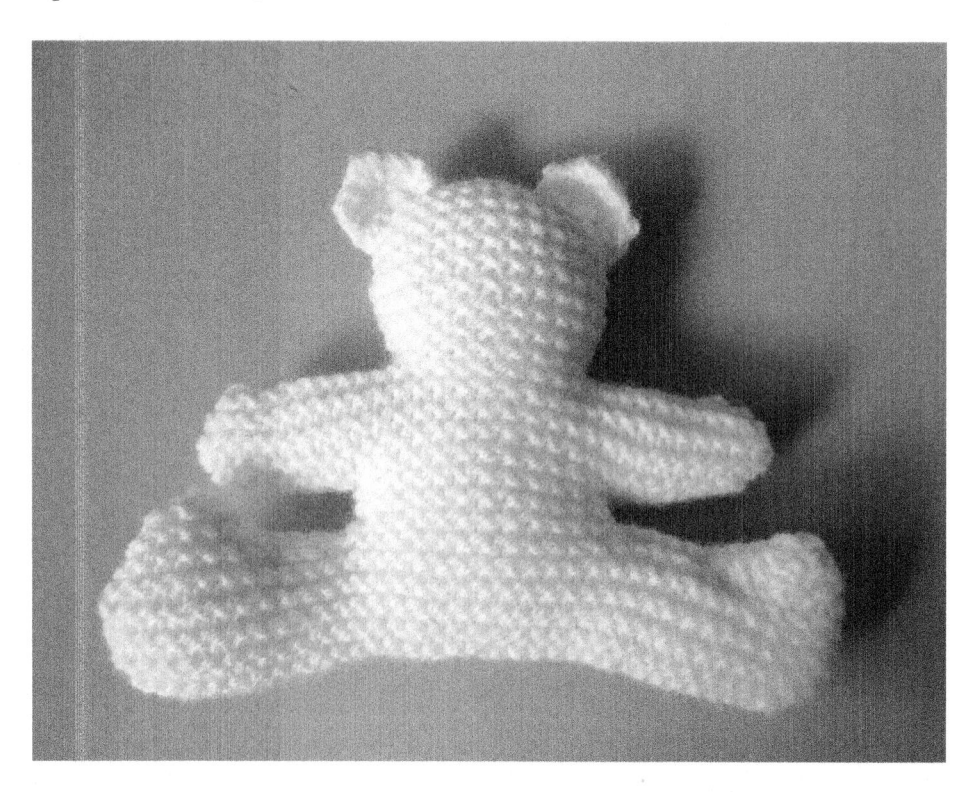

Christmas Cat Knitting Projects

Sew a gathering thread around the neck & tighten to define the head from the body a bit more.

Ears - With 3.25mm needles cast on 8sts.

Garter St 4 rows.

Decrease each end of every row until 4 sts remain.

Cast Off.

Hat - The hat is quite large & slouchy to go over one ear.

With 4mm needles & brim colour cast on 24sts.

Garter st 3 rows.

Change to hat colour & St st 8 rows.

Next row - K2, (k2 tog, k4) to last 2 sts, k2.

St st 3 rows.

*Next row - K2, (k2tog, k3) to last 3sts, k2tog, k1.

St st 3 rows.

Next row - (K2 k2tog) to end.

Christmas Cat Knitting Projects

St st 3 rows.

Next row - (K2, k2tog) to end.

St st 3 rows.

Next row - (K1, k2 tog) to end.

P 1 row.

*Next row -K2 tog to end.

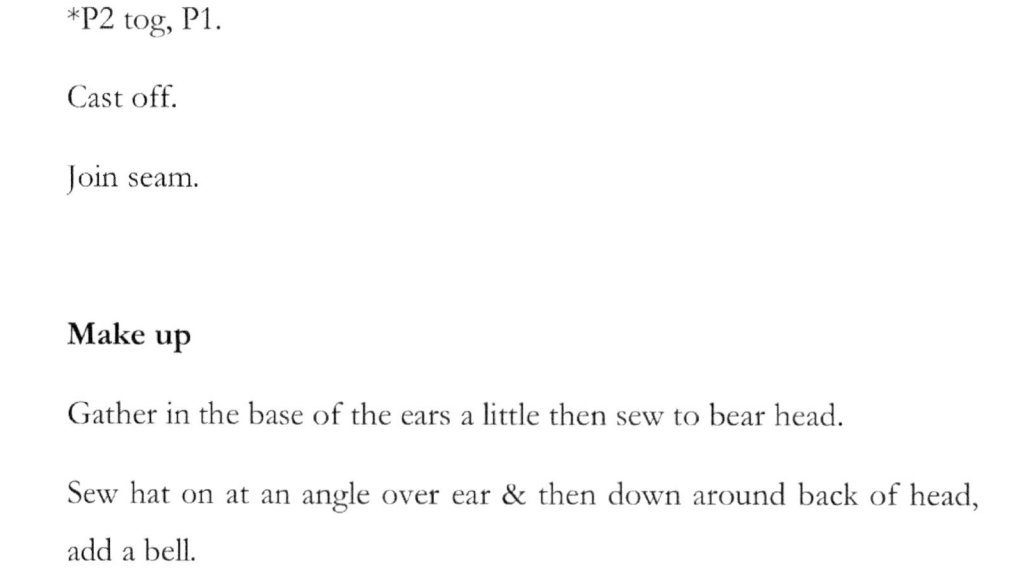

*P2 tog, P1.

Cast off.

Join seam.

Make up

Gather in the base of the ears a little then sew to bear head.

Sew hat on at an angle over ear & then down around back of head, add a bell.

Using 3 strands of black embroidery cotton sew in paws. Sew on beads for eyes & sew on nose & mouth.

To glue to bauble

I use gold thread through the top of the head to hang them, instead of using the hanger on the bauble. If you want to hang it from the bauble make sure you glue the hanger on the bauble as close to the bear body as you can, or else the weight of the bear will make them hang "back heavy" (if that makes sense).

Check first the bear is not over stuffed. You need to be able to bend it around & glue the paws in place without much resistance. See photo, glue bauble on an angle so the hanger is to the side of the face. Put glue on the bear, not the bauble. Start by putting a little on the tummy to hold the bauble in place. Glue the paws into place, but make sure you put the glue at least 1cm back from the edge of the paw as it will spread when pressed. Hold each paw a few moments while the glue sets, before doing the next one.

Christmas Cat Knitting Projects

Cat

Same as the bear but with the whole back done in 4row stripes. The front is striped until you get to the head, then all white from there.

Ears

With 3.25mm needles & orange cast on 8sts.

Garter st 2 rows.

Decrease each end of every row until 2 stitches remain

K2 tog fasten off.

All done.

Christmas Cat Knitting Projects

Santa Cat Hat

Materials

- 30 yards of Cascade Eco Wool (white)

- 40 yards of Cascade 220 (red)

- 1 US size 7 16 inch circular needles OR needle size needed to achieve gauge.

- 1 US size 7 circular needles, any length, OR needle size needed to achieve gauge

Christmas Cat Knitting Projects

(US size 7 DPNs may also be used instead of 2 circular needles)

- Row counter

- Tapestry needle

Special Skills Needed

- Knitting in the round using two circular needles

Gauge

- 4.5 stitches = 1 inch on US size 7 needles in stockinette stitch with Cascade 220

- 3.5 stitches = 1 inch on US size 7 needles in seed stitch with Cascade Eco

Finished Measurements

Finished hat circumference is 15 inches at the brim. Please note that my cat has an enormous head!

Christmas Cat Knitting Projects

Abbreviations

[ ] repeat instructions between bracketsco cast on

k knit

k2tog knit two stitches together

pm place marker

sts stitch(es)

Directions

Loosely CO 56 sts on one circular needle (needle A) using the white yarn. Slip half of the stitches to the other circular needle (needle B). Join to knit in the round, placing a marker at that point so you know where the round begins. Since my cat has an enormous head, you can create a smaller hat by casting on less stitches in multiples of 7 (example: cast on 49 stitches or 42 stitches).

Brim

Round 1: [k1, p1] to end

Round 2: [p1, k1] to end

Repeat rounds 1 and 2 three more times for a total of 8 rounds.

Hat

Switch to the red yarn.

Rounds 1-5: knit all sts

Round 6: [k5, k2tog] to end. 48 sts

Rounds 7-11: knit all sts

Round 12: [k4, k2tog] to end. 40 sts

Rounds 13-17: knit all sts

Round 18: [k3, k2tog] to end. 32 sts

Rounds 19-23: knit all sts

Round 24: [k2, k2tog] to end. 24 sts

Rounds 25-29: knit all sts

Round 30: [k4, k2tog] to end. 20 sts

Rounds 31-35: knit all sts

Round 36: [k3, k2tog] to end. 16 sts

Round 37-41: knit all sts

Round 42: [k2, k2tog] to end. 12 sts

Rounds 43-44: knit all sts

Round 45: [k1, k2tog] to end. 8 sts

Rounds 46-47: knit all sts

Round 48: [k2tog] to end. 4 sts

Cut yarn, leaving a 6 inch tail.

Finishing

Using the tapestry needle, thread the yarn tail through the 4 remaining sts. Pull closed. Weave in ends. Make a 2-inch pom pom using the white yarn and sew it to the top of the hat.

Christmas Cat Knitting Projects

Santa Claws Cat

Materials

- 30 yards of Cascade Eco Wool (white)

- 40 yards of Cascade 220 (red)

- 1 US size 7 16 inch circular needles OR needle size needed to achieve gauge.

Christmas Cat Knitting Projects

- 1 US size 7 circular needles, any length, OR needle size needed to achieve gauge
- Row counter
- Tapestry needle

Instructions

Cast on 40 stitches in CC (white?) and knit three rows of garter in the round (remember, garter in the round is knit one row, purl one row).

Before you start row 4, split your stitches onto two needles. Working back and forth:

Row 4: SSK, knit to two stitches before end of row, K2Tog

Row 5: Purl across

Complete these two rows once more. Switch to MC (I'm going to guess you chose red) and:

Row 8: Knit across

Row 9: Purl across

Row 10: SSK, knit to two stitches before end of row, K2Tog

Row 11: Purl across

Complete these four rows once more.

Complete rows 4-11 for the stitches on the other needle. You should have 24 stitches between the two needles but don't take my word for it.

Divide the stitches evenly between 3 needles; you'll be working in the round now. On the second needle, place a marker in between where the stitches of the flaps don't yet connect between the 12th and 13th stitch.

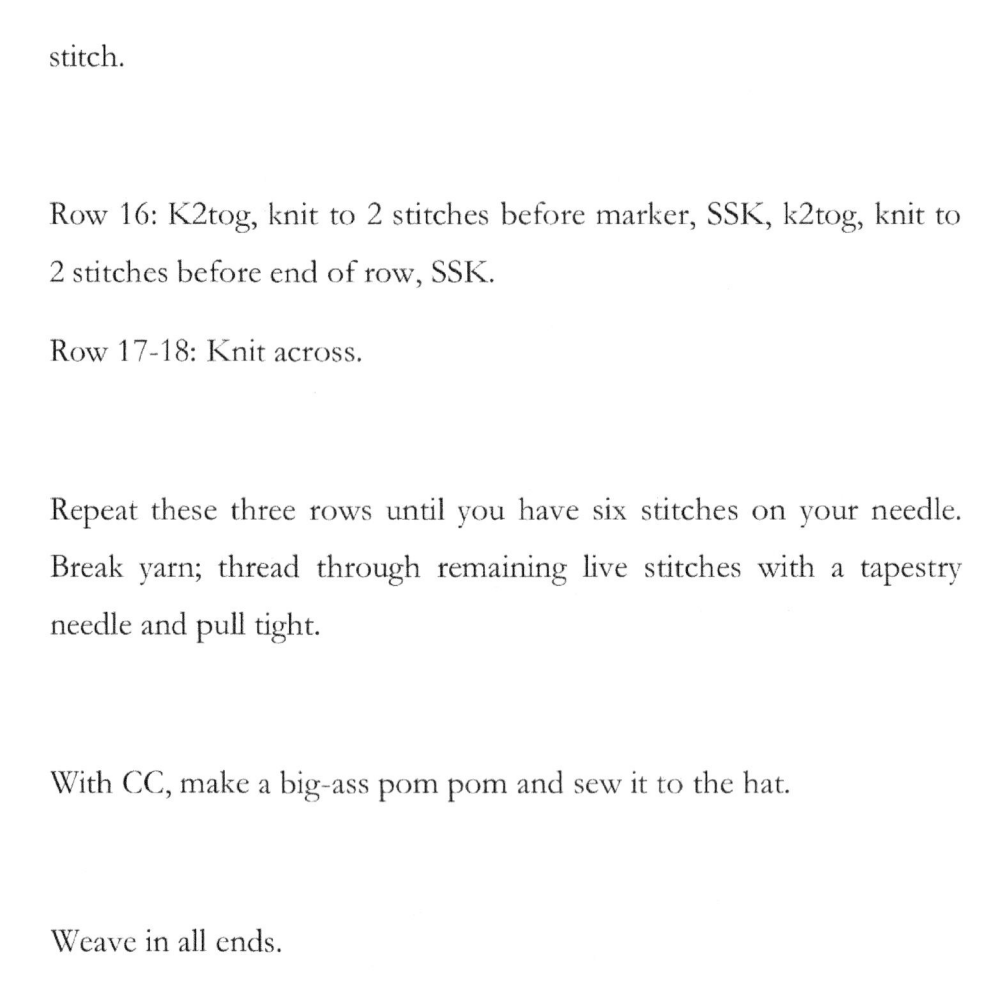

Row 16: K2tog, knit to 2 stitches before marker, SSK, k2tog, knit to 2 stitches before end of row, SSK.

Row 17-18: Knit across.

Repeat these three rows until you have six stitches on your needle. Break yarn; thread through remaining live stitches with a tapestry needle and pull tight.

With CC, make a big-ass pom pom and sew it to the hat.

Weave in all ends.

Christmas Cat Knitting Projects

Happy Knitting!

Christmas Cat Knitting Projects

Cat Scarf Knitting Pattern

Christmas Cat Knitting Projects

SUPPLIES:

US 13 straight needles

Appox 25 yards of super bulky yarn (pictured yarn is Lion brand Wool Ease Thick and Quick)

3/4 inch or 1 inch button (don't go any bigger than this or your button won't slip through the stitches.

Needle and thread

GAUGE: 2 stitches = 1 inch (don't worry if this is off slightly)

3 Sizes: Young Cat (6-12 months), Small/Medium Adult Cat, and Large Adult Cat

PATTERN:

With the US 13 needles cast on

3 stitches (Young Cat: Age 6-12 months)

4 stitches (All Adult Cats)

Knit back and forth in row until work measures

16 inches (Young Cat) pictured

19 inches (Small, Medium Cat)

20 inches (Large cat) pictured

Bind off all stitches. Weave in all ends. Sew a button onto the scarf 3 inches from end (young cat), 4 inches from end (small, medium cat) 4 1/2 inches from end (large cat). Curve the scarf around your cats neck and push the button up through the stitching to secure. Be careful to not make it too tight for your furry friend!

Easy Cat Toy Knitting Pattern

Needles: Size US 3 single point knitting needles

Also needed: yarn needle, fiber fill, catnip

Gauge: Not important for this project

Cast on 20 sts.

Christmas Cat Knitting Projects

Row 1: k1, ssk, k22, m1, k1

Row 2: Knit across.

Repeat these 2 rows for 28 rows. Bind off.

How to finish the cat toy

Once you have binded off, bring the edges together and sew the seam closed.

Make a running stitch along the bottom, pull to gather and secure.

Christmas Cat Knitting Projects

Stuff the ball with fiber fill and catnip (use approximately 1 ½ tablespoons per ball).

Make another stitch along the top, pull to gather and secure.

Christmas Cat Knitting Projects

Knit Cat Mini Christmas Sleep Stockings

HOW TO KNIT EASY MINI CHRISTMAS STOCKINGS

Yarn: any #4 weight yarn

Needles: Size US 7 single point knitting needles

Christmas Cat Knitting Projects

Size: Approximately 5 inches tall

With the white yarn, cast on 18 sts.

Cuff:

Switch color. Knit for 5 rows.

Body:

Knit 12 rows in Stockinette Stitch.

Shape heel:

Knit 10 – Turn

Purl 3 – Turn

Knit 4 – Turn

Purl 5 – Turn

Knit 6 – Turn

Christmas Cat Knitting Projects

Purl 7 – Turn

Knit 8 – Turn

Purl 9 – Turn

Knit 10 – Turn

Purl to the end of the row.

Toe:

(Right side) Work 6 rows in stockinette Stitch

Next row: K2 tog, K1 across row (12 stitches)

Next row: Purl

Next row: K2 tog across row (6 stitches)

Break yarn, leaving a long tail. Pull through remaining stitches and pull to tighten. Fold stocking over and sew seam. Weave in ends.

Christmas Cat Knitting Projects

Make Your Own Knit Cat Bed

Supplies:

Christmas Cat Knitting Projects

-400-600 yards extra bulky craft yarn. I used about 400 yards of this yarn in cilantro—you may use more if you have a bigger cat.

–10mm knitting needles

–A darning needle

This bed is knit with two strands of yarn held together as one (also called plying) to give the feel and appearance of bulkier yarn. Wind two skeins into one big ball of yarn by holding two strands together and rolling away, which leaves you with one extra thick strand. You can just use two strands straight from the skein, but I find that things get tangled that way.

Cast on 28 stitches, leaving a two-foot tail, and start knitting a garter stitch. See how the two strands together make one functional strand? Keep on knitting, and come back when you've done about 60 rows.

Christmas Cat Knitting Projects

Here's where you can adjust the size of the bed based on your cat's size. Hold the short ends of your rectangle end to end—this is roughly the circumference of the finished bed. Start checking for size around 60 rows, and keep knitting until the bed is as big as you want it. I stopped around 65 rows because Bisou likes her beds pretty snug (she's 9 lbs. for reference). A bigger cat might need a 70-80 row bed.

Christmas Cat Knitting Projects

When you're ready, cast off. You should have a very long, simple rectangle like this one. Tie off and trim leftover yarn, but leave the tails you made when you cast on.

Christmas Cat Knitting Projects

Make a loop by attaching the short ends of the rectangle to each other. Use the darning needle and one of the long tails to sew the sides together, pulling the tail tightly through the end stitches for a snug seam.

Christmas Cat Knitting Projects

Once the sides are sewn together, stitch one more loop and pull the tail through the loop. Tighten and trim the excess yarn.

Christmas Cat Knitting Projects

Now that you have a big loop, it's time to cinch one of the ends (the one with the remaining tail) together to form the middle of the bed. Weave the tail through every other stitch along the edge of the loop as shown.

Christmas Cat Knitting Projects

Cinch as you go by pulling on the yarn as tightly as you can! You want a really tight cinch with no hole in the middle, so tighten then tighten some more. Once the whole edge is cinched, make another loop, thread the tail, tighten and trim the excess yarn.

Christmas Cat Knitting Projects

Do you have a giant beanie? Okay, just one more step!

Push the cinched part down—this is now the center of the bed. Pull the sides up and fold them over so the bed looks like this. It's kitty ready!

Christmas Cat Knitting Projects

Happy Knitting!

Christmas Cat Knitting Projects

Fair Isle Mice – Pattern For Cat

To make your own mice, you will need:

Oddments of double knitting weight yarn in main colour and 5 contrasting colours

A pair of 3.75 needles

Toy stuffing

Christmas Cat Knitting Projects

ABBREVIATIONS

k = knit

p = purl

sts = stitches

inc = increase

k2tog = knit 2 sts together

k2togtbl = knit 2 sts together through the back of the loops

Finished size – 3 inches long (excluding tail)

BODY

(Starting at tail end of mouse)

With main shade and 3.75mm needles cast on 9 sts, leaving a long end to make tail.

Row 1: k 1, inc knitwise in every st to end. (17 sts)

Row 2: p

Row 3: k 1, inc knitwise in every st to end. (33 sts)

Row 4: p

Row 5: k

Row 6: p

Rows 7 – 13: work Fair Isle pattern from chart.

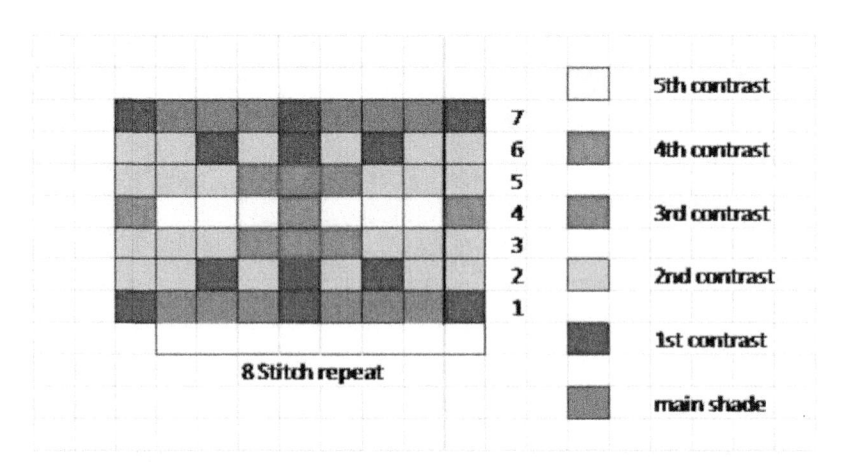

Row 14: p

Row 15: K2tog, k 8, k2tog, k 9, k2togtbl, k 8, k2togtbl. (29 sts)

Row 16: p

Row 17: K2tog, k 7, k2tog, k 7, k2togtbl, k 7, k2togtbl. (25 sts)

Row 18: p

Row 19: K2tog, k 6, k2tog, k 5, k2togtbl, k 6, k2togtbl. (21 sts)

Row 20: p

Row 21: K2tog, k 4, k2tog, k 5, k2togtbl, k 4, k2togtbl. (17 sts)

Row 22: p

Row 23: K2tog, k 3, k2tog, k 3, k2togtbl, k 3, k2togtbl. (13 sts)

Row 24: p

Row 25: K2tog, k 2, k2tog, k 1, k2togtbl, k 2, k2togtbl. (9 sts)

Break off yarn and thread through remaining sts and pull up tight. Fasten off.

Christmas Cat Knitting Projects

EARS (make 2)

With main shade and 3.75mm needles cast on 3 sts.

Row 1: inc knitwise in every st. (6 sts)

Row 2: k

Row 3: k

Christmas Cat Knitting Projects

Row 4: k

Row 5: k2tog, k 2, k2togtbl. (4 sts)

Row 6: k2tog, k2togtbl. (2 sts)

Row 7: k2tog.

Fasten off.

MAKING UP

Sew up seam on body and stuff.

With the long tail from the cast on, make a twisted cord of about 5 inches in length to form the tail.

Attach the ears to the head and embroider eyes.

Printed in Great Britain
by Amazon